F

A Complete Guide to Real Reiki

Contents

INTRODUCTION

Before we begin with Reiki and how it can be used, I would urge you to take a deep breath….close your eyes…relax …… and allow your mind to visualize.

Let your mind visualize the power that you have:

The immense power to miraculously heal yourself and people around you!

The unlimited power that helps you unlock the secret to eternal happiness and bliss!

The power that ensures ample healing energy runs through your hands and helps you ease physical pain as well as mental stress!

The power that provides you with the magical ability to become your own spiritual doctor and hence work your own miracles!

Alright…alright….I can read all that! **But how is all this possible?** How can I become a spiritual doctor or experience eternal happiness without any external support?

Well... that is what this book is about.

This book is your guide to eternal happiness, success and healing – all through use of one simple thing called **love**.

But I thought this book was about Reiki?

True – and Reiki is all about bringing healing through compassion and unconditional love.

So, is Reiki not something religious?

Well, Reiki is immensely spiritual in nature. However, it is not considered a religion. In fact, it is often regarded as a form of alternative medicine.

From a traditional standpoint Reiki means 'life force energy' or 'spiritual energy.' The word Reiki traces its origin in two words:

1. Rei implying universal and

2. Ki implying life force or life energy. This is the energy that constitutes everything in this universe.

Reiki practitioners use the five principles of Reiki in order to act as channels for healing energies. This healing energy typically flows through the practitioner's body, hands and then into the body where their hands are touching to help eradicate disease and misery using the power of unconditional love.

The best part – practitioners can treat themselves too!

By simply using the power of unconditional love that allows healing energies to flow through their hands.

Excited to know and discover more?

Let's get started….

WHAT IS REIKI?

I will describe Reiki as a healing technique that utilizes the power of touch to heal your own self or heal others. Apart from healing, Reiki is also used as a method that helps you attain mental and physical balance.

It can be explained as a non-invasive method to endorse relaxation, elevate the natural remedial abilities of the human body and nurture physical, emotional, mental and spiritual well-being. The therapeutic energy of Reiki is generally applied to deliver relief from illnesses such as anxiety, aches and pains, fatigue, anxiety and other physical and mental ailments. It does not replace any form of treatment, but simply acts as a complimentary therapy that can be integrated with any treatment to boost internal health and well-being.

As already mentioned, the word Reiki is derived from two words:

- Rei which implies universal and
- Ki which means life force or life energy. This is the energy that constitutes everything in this universe.

Rei can also be defined as *"the Higher Intelligence that guides the creation and functioning of the universe.*" It is a subtle wisdom that permeates everything, animate as well as inanimate. This subtle wisdom controls the development of the entire universe – ranging from the development of life on this planet to the unfolding of galaxies in the universe. Its presence guides you whenever you need it.

Ki can be termed as the non-physical energy that is present in all living things. Ki flows in every living thing – including human beings, plants and animals. An individual feels strong and confident when he has a high Ki. A low Ki leads to a feeling of sickness and ill health. You receive this Ki from your food, air, sunshine and even sleep. You also have the potential to elevate the level of Ki in your body through specific breathing and meditation exercises. An individual's Ki leaves his physical body at the time of his death. Ki is also known as "Prana" in India, "Chi" in China, the "Ti" or "Ki' in the Hawaiians. It is also referred to as the life force, vital energy force, orgone, odic force, or bioplasma.

One of the most important characteristics of Ki is the potential to respond to your feelings and thoughts. Ki is either weakened or begins to flow with greater strength depending on your feelings, emotions and thoughts. Negative feelings and thoughts can lead to a restricted Ki.

The secret to Reiki healing is that the practitioner transfers this healing energy directly into the patient by connecting him unshakably to the supreme universal energy. This energy moves from the healer into the recipient.

Alright, so the healer transfers his energy into the recipient. In this case, wouldn't he experience a diminishing energy?

Absolutely not!

This healing energy is never depleted and is in fact utilized to heal and energize the healer. Another great thing about this energy is that it travels where it is needed most, implying that this is one of the most intelligent forms of energy that can never be misused or abused and naturally flows in the direction it is required to flow in. This also means that this energy does not require any deliberate direction by the healer.

A number of people wonder about the manner in which this energy flows. I mean…imagine Universal Life force energy flowing from the hands of the practitioner to the patient.…*How is it possible?*

Along with the physical elements such as organs, organ systems, nerves, glands, arteries, muscles, bones, etc., your body possesses a subtle energy system through which your vital 'life force energy' flows. This vital life force energy comprises of energy bodies that engulf your physical body and help you to process your emotions, thoughts and ideas. Each energy body is linked to an energy center which is referred to as the chakra. The chakras work like valves that enable this energy to pass through your spiritual, mental, physical and emotional being. Your body also possesses energy meridians which function like a river carrying this energy through your body, nourishing it and balancing your physical system, mental function and spiritual purpose.

You are healthy and alive because of the presence of this *'life force energy'*. A blockage in this energy leads to sickness and ill-health. Stress often weakens the flow of this energy and is also the leading cause of a number of lifestyle disorders.

Reiki induces a feeling of pure relaxation and thereby addresses the root cause of your weakened energy system. It reinstates the energy balance in your body and fills you with vigor and vitality by getting rid of the physical and emotional impact of this unreleased stress. It opens your blocked meridians and chakras very gently, yet powerfully. It clears your energy bodies and leaves you with a feeling of ultimate relaxation and peace.

According to the wisdom of Reiki and yogic sciences, disease is present in the seed form in our causal body. When it remains unchecked, it manifests as conscious or subconscious thoughts in our mental body. Gradually, it takes an emotional thought form and then, an energy form.

From that point onwards, if it is not checked, it takes a physical form where it is manifested in the physical world and you can see and feel it. There are multiple opportunities to correct the disease. If you are able to remove all the seeds of disease from your causal body, then the manifestation into mental or emotional energies and physical bodies will not happen. Or if you are able to put a check on our thoughts, they will act as a filter and not let any thought of disease reach to the grosser layers of emotions and energy. The power of Reiki works on all of these layers at the same time.

It heals your causal body spiritually. The thoughts that you experience during your Reiki practice have the potential to heal your mental and emotional bodies and of course, wherever this Reiki power is applied, it attracts and harmonizes all the needed energies at that particular point.

It is important to understand that this particular point does not have to be a point in the physical body, it could just be a concept or an event – depending on your intention. The important thing is that whenever you apply Reiki power to this point, it has the potential to attract the right type and amount of energies for this point.

This energy can then heal the situation or in this case the point in the body. This further explains the versatility of Reiki where it addresses the full personality – not just the physical, mental or emotional aspect but even the deeper recesses of your mind through regular practice are healed. This gift of Reiki is not available in any other healing technique.

In terms of physical healing, Reiki boosts up the process of healing, helps in cleansing of toxins and releases energy blockages which help the person connect with their internal healer.

In order to understand the process of Chi depletion, imagine yourself as a new car, representing a young individual. This car is capable of charging its battery all by itself, simply by running around. And the battery remains in a perfectly healthy state irrespective of the weather conditions. However, as time passes, the process of aging sets in. The car starts experiencing damaged parts and is unable to hold its charge well. It runs well in summers or in less demanding conditions. However, it demonstrates major breakdowns during demanding conditions such as the rainy or the winter season.

Your body experiences similar things. Just like the battery of the car, your body runs really well in your childhood, teenage and early adulthood. The burden of responsibilities, family, job, mortgage, kids and other relationships sets in the cycle of stress. And then, it needs charging!

This charge is provided through an external source via Reiki treatment. The battery charger is your Universal Life Force Energy or Reiki.

And without this life force energy, you experience powerlessness, helplessness and ultimately, lifelessness!

*So, we can also say that Reiki is the '**Healing power of Divine Grace and a methodical way to channel it as unconditional love**.'*

And what happens in a typical Reiki session?

Well, in a typical Reiki session, the person getting Reiki stays fully dressed and rests on a comfortable table as the Reiki practitioner or expert lightly moves their hands over the patient. Typical sessions last for around an hour and leave the patient relaxed and destressed. Shorter therapies can also be provided in a lounge chair or your own bed.

A typical session would also feel like a warm ray of sunlight that has a comforting impact on your body, mind and spirit as it flows around you. This also implies that Reiki has a holistic impact – it impacts your mind, body and spirit. Another important characteristic about Reiki is its ability to be extremely nurturing and yet immensely powerful.

ADVANTAGES OF USING REIKI AS A SYSTEM OF HEALING

When we compare Reiki to other alternative therapies, it demonstrates some clear benefits:

- Reiki involves transfer of universal life force energy from the practitioner to the person getting initiated. As mentioned previously, this is an intelligent energy that recognizes your weak zones and helps in correcting all imbalances in your body.

- Reiki is simple – anyone can learn and practice this system of healing. More so, it can be used for healing your own self as well as healing others.

- Reiki is safe – this energy can be used only for good. There is absolutely no risk of this energy falling into wrong hands and subsequently being used for evil. This intelligent energy does not work if the person practicing it has evil intentions.

- The Reiki healing system is simple and uncomplicated – it only involves intention and unconditional love to heal. You do not need any complicated tools to practice it.

- If you have been initiated into Reiki once, it implies that you have been initiated into Reiki for a lifetime. You do not need to repeat the process and can continue using it for a lifetime.

- Reiki is not connected to any particular religion. Therefore, anyone can practice it irrespective of the religious beliefs a person follows.

- Healing by Reiki does not involve any kind of manipulation of the body using massage or force. It only involves gentle placing of hands on a person's body or may be a few inches above it.

THE FIVE REIKI PRINCIPLES

The foundation of Reiki rests in understanding and mastering the principles that guide its existence. A thorough understanding of these five principles can help a person in substantially developing their own technique. These principles are in reality the guiding principles that explain how one should conduct themselves in their day to day life. Here are the five principles of Reiki that have their roots in the teachings of Usui Sensei:

- "Just for today: I will live in the attitude of gratitude.

- Just for today: I will not worry.

- Just for today: I will not be angry.

- Just for today: I will be honest to my own self.

- Just for today: I will respect all living beings."

The essence of Reiki as explained by these principles is mentioned below:

JUST FOR TODAY: The importance of 'today' is highlighted in all five principles. Today defines your present. It teaches you to live each and every moment of the day completely – it just becomes a collection of moments. It is easier to make a commitment to these principles for one day at a time rather than making a lofty commitment to follow these throughout your life to come. You will find more success when you affirm and commit to these principles on a daily basis.

I WILL LIVE IN THE ATTITUDE OF GRATITUDE: Reiki encourages you to be thankful, receiving and giving the gift of the universe. You should be thankful about everything in your life – the good, the bad and the ugly. Being thankful breaks the cycle of misery. If you are going through a bad time, or suffering, then it is because of some karma which was performed in the past which has become the cause of suffering today. If you start brooding over this and blaming others, you just sink deeper into that misery. By being thankful for whatever you have and whatever situation you are in, you break the cycle of misery – you break the influence of that effect and gradually that thought process leads you out of the suffering that you are in. It initiates a new cause for good things to happen in your life.

I WILL NOT FEAR OR WORRY: The principles of Reiki encourage you to trust the universe completely. They tell you to let go of your fears and worries, make the best possible efforts and leave the rest in the hands of the universe. This frees you from your fears and you start believing in the universe.

Fear begets more fear, worry begets more worry. The moment you stop worrying, you demonstrate your faith on the Absolute and the moment that demonstration happens, the powers of Reiki descend on you and begin to support you. So, don't let fear create more fear and don't let worry create more worry. Just for today, live without fear or worry.

I WILL NOT BE ANGRY: This principle encourages you to stay away from anger and attain perfect balance of emotion and mind through Reiki. It guides you to live a peaceful and a quiet life.

Anger burns your positive karma and reduces the power of your soul. In some cases, you can be angry about rightful causes. Positive anger is sometimes good, however, it has to be channeled correctly. And in all circumstances it is better to not be angry and think about the situation in a positive manner. This does not mean that you become inert and not respond to a situation – it simply means that you act with peace and understanding of the situation that you are in. That is the best way to not burn your positive karma and use it to your advantage.

I WILL BE HONEST TO MY OWN SELF: Reiki shows you how to integrate and utilize the power of honesty for everyday work. It reiterates the importance of work and how working honestly can enable you to lead a meaningful life, growing and learning every day!

Honesty towards your own self is extremely important. When you are honest to your own self, you increase the power of your soul and let it work through your mind and body. When you are not honest with your own self, you disintegrate. Your chakras start to fall out of alignment and you are not able to draw the right amount of power from your soul into your mind. And this dishonesty to your own self weakens your mind and the power of your soul. Yoga is about alignment and integration of all the chakras into this higher chakra and the first step to do this is by being honest to your own self.

I WILL BE RESPECTFUL OF MY PARENTS AND ELDERS: Over a period of time, this has been expanded into '***Just for today, I will be respectful of all living beings***.' Whatever learning you have achieved is because of your parents and elders, and also people around you. When you interact with people, you learn some things, you share some good experiences, some bad experiences – you need to respect people for all that they are teaching you. This respect also empowers you to see everybody as your own extended self. This does not mean that you should not be cautious and that you should not apply your judgment when interacting with people – it just means that you act with respect under all circumstances and that you are never hateful or spiteful.

Reiki encourages you to nurture a sense of oneness and love. It mentions that there is one single soul in this universe and this soul does not distinguish between self and others. Therefore, when you are kind to others, you are kind to yourself!

THE THREE PILLARS OF REIKI

Ussui Sensei also mentions about the three pillars of Reiki. These are:

- Your body is your 'Temple of the Spirit'; and it is your responsibility to treat it with respect and care for it. Usui himself practiced Kiko in order to gain strength and suppleness and refill his own Ki. You should also practice Tai Chi, Yoga etc. in order to maintain perfect health and wellness. You should also receive Reiki from others at frequent intervals.

- You are also encouraged to look after your mind. Usui looked after his mind meditating every day. Meditation should be a part of your lifestyle too, especially due to the demands laid by the stressful lifestyle of today.

- You should focus on caring for the society by giving Reiki to others. Always remember that Reiki flows through you. Therefore, the more you care for others and treat others through Reiki, the more you benefit.

REIKI ATTUNEMENTS

Before you can seek Reiki treatments, your practitioner will need to initiate the attunement process. This process opens the chakras in your body and establishes an exceptional connection between the Reiki source and the student (in this case, you).

The Reiki attunement process is an extremely impactful spiritual experience that involves channelization of energies into the student through the medium of a Reiki Master. It helps to connect the student to the Reiki energy source. This process is monitored by the Rei or God-consciousness that helps in making adjustments in the process based on the specific requirements of each student. Various Reiki guides and spiritual gurus are present during the process of attunement and they enable the student to implement the process. You may experience some personal messages, past life experiences, specific healings, sound and vision or any other kind of mystical experiences during or after this process.

The process of attunement may elevate your psychic sensitivity and you may experience increased intuitive awareness, opening of the third eye, or any other psychic ability after receiving a Reiki attunement.

Having received Reiki attunement means that Reiki stays with you throughout your life. You will never lose it and it will never wear off. You typically require one attunement to reach a particular level; however additional attunements may bring greater benefits including refinement of the Reiki energy you are channeling, an elevated strength of energy, clarity of mind, healing of personal problems, and enhanced level of consciousness and increased psychic sensitivity.

The process of Reiki attunement initiates a cleansing process that impacts your emotions, body and mind. It empowers you to release the stored toxins and harmful chemicals from your body and initiates a process of purification. In fact, a specific process of purification is recommended prior to an attunement process. This enhances the results of your attunement process.

In order to prepare yourself for the attunement process, you may want to find an instructor. As you begin your search, you may realize that there are several instructors to choose from – and then you may have to narrow down your list!

You do want to take special care in selecting the best possible instructor available in your area. You need to be really comfortable in their presence. Your instructor (who will be called as a 'Reiki master') will be able to teach you how to use Reiki during your attunement. *The attunement process will help you switch on your infinite supply of life force energy.*

Once you book an appointment for Reiki attunement, you will need to purify your body. This is done to allow the seamless flow of energy through your body.

Here are the specific steps that you can follow prior to the process of attunement:

- You should refrain from consuming fish or meat for at least three days prior to your attunement. Various drugs such as penicillin, certain female hormones, toxins such as pesticides and certain heavy metals that throw your system out of balance and make you sluggish are present in these products. This interferes with the process of attunement.

- You may want to consider fasting as a method of detoxification. A juice fast or water fast three days prior to your attunement can work like magic.

- You may want to refrain from consumption of alcohol for at least three days prior to your attuncment process.

- You should also reduce your consumption of tea or coffee. If possible, stop drinking tea or coffee completely. This is because caffeine is known to create an imbalance in your nervous system.

- You may want to reduce the use of sweets. It is recommended that you do not consume chocolate three days prior to the attunement process.

- Are you a smoker? It is advisable to reduce the number of cigarettes you consume and to not smoke at all on the day of your attunement.

- One week prior to the process of attunement, start the process of meditation (in case you do not practice it already). It is recommended that you spend at least one hour in perfect silence or practicing a form of meditation that you are familiar with. Practice this every day, starting seven days prior to your attunement.

- Do not watch television, read newspapers or listen to the radio. Cut back on this time at least a week before your attunement.

- Do not participate in any activity that drains your energy.

- Try spending time with yourself, moderate exercise and nature walks. Begin this a week prior to your attunement.

- Start giving attention to details. Everything around you sends a subtle message, try and spend time in interpreting their meaning.

- You are encouraged to create a sacred space inside you and eliminate hatred, jealousy, fear, worry, anger, hatred etc.

- Cleanse your aura before the attunement class.

- Always try and stay hydrated by drinking plenty of water.

- Also, try and get a good night's sleep the night before the class. If you were not fasting, eat a light but nourishing breakfast on the day of your class.

The attunement process will be carried out in a quite setting as this helps in getting the best possible results. Your Reiki instructor or master will ask you to lie down on a flat surface (mostly a massage table). Let go of all the anger, hatred, jealousy, etc. as you begin the process of attunement.

THE INITIATION PROCESS

Now that your body is prepared for the purpose of attunement, you will need to go through an initiation ceremony. The process of attunement will be unique to you. It is a surreal experience that cannot be described in words. The only thing that is required of you is to be fully present and attentive during the entire experience. It is best to keep your eyes closed which helps in building focus and concentration. During the process of attunement, you can also expect to hear some mantras which will help you to connect with the universal life force energy in a better manner.

A number of different symbols will be used in the attunement process. These symbols are not only used in the attunement process but also in performing Reiki treatments. These symbols are energized by the practitioner as they focus on the intention.

Here are some of the symbols that are typically used in the Reiki attunement process:

Power Reiki symbol:

The Japanese name for this symbol is 'Cho Ku Rei' implying – 'I have the key'. The main use of this symbol is to increase or decrease power. It draws energy from around you and then enables you to focus that energy on the destination that you have assigned for it. Reversing the symbol can decrease the power, in which case it will leave the Reiki master and manifest in yourself.

Harmony Reiki symbol:

The Japanese name for this symbol is 'SeiHei Ki' implying 'Key to the Universe'. It represents harmony and is often referred to as the peacemaker symbol. Most Reiki practitioners use this symbol with an intent to purify – it is said that this symbol helps in levelling the playing field when you are going through a tough time in life.

Connection Reiki Symbol:

The Japanese name for this symbol is 'Hon Sha ZeShoNen'. This is referred to as the Distance symbol since it is used to send Reiki to long distances. It looks like a tower and means – 'The God in me greets the God in you to promote peace and enlightenment.'

Balancing Reiki Symbol:

This symbol helps in balancing all energy that is produced during a Reiki session. It is called 'Tam A Ra Sha' and is helpful in unblocking the chakras.

Master Reiki Symbol:

The Japanese name for this symbol is 'Dai KoMyo.' This symbol is the heart of Reiki and is used to represent everything that is Reiki. The only purpose of this symbol is to reiterate the fact that Reiki is available to anyone who believes in unconditional love. It is a power that works directly with the soul and facilitates healing.

Completion Reiki Symbol:

The Japanese name for this symbol is Raku. It is also known as a fire serpent and represents your 'chi' or life force energy.

During your Reiki initiation session, all the above symbols will need to be activated. Reiki masters can choose various methods to activate the symbols depending on the intent that they are using the symbol for.

Once the symbols have been activated, they can be applied to specific areas of the body in order to create the desired impact.

Once the attunement process is complete, you will begin to find a release from various ties that had bound you to your past behaviors. You will now be considered at par with the group of individuals who utilize the power of Reiki to heal themselves, each other and the environment. You will be able to identify the source of your energy and in case you see this source as negative energy, you will be able to eliminate it.

Once you begin with Reiki, you will also be amazed at the ease with which you are able to make changes to your normal routine.

Here are some of the things that can help you get past a few difficult days:

Journaling: Journaling always helps. Write down all your experiences in order to avoid blocking your energy. Remember, pent up energy may impact your well-being.

Discussions: If there are things that you need more clarity on, seek support from your Reiki master. If you need to talk about your experiences, find another student who is walking the same path. Discussion with them will help you discover new methods of coping up with the aftermath, where your feelings are awakened beyond imagination.

Believe: Believe in yourself, believe in Reiki! Even if you are feeling terrible initially, your belief will help you get through. The emotional turmoil that you are going through may simply be necessary to open doors for better well-being.

THE SEVEN CHAKRAS AND REIKI

Heard about chakras?

The chakras are the energy centers of the body. They are often called the seven vortexes of energy spinning inside your body. These vortexes of energy are placed along your spine beginning from the bottom of your pelvis and moving up to the crown of your head.

And these chakras can reveal more information about you than anything or anybody else can.

When you gain an understanding about your chakras, you gain an understanding about your own self.

Harnessing the power of chakras can enable you to draw maximum benefits for yourself. Understanding the chakras helps you understand why you feel an imbalance, when you feel an imbalance and how can you overcome that imbalance through the power of your spinning energy wheels.

With Reiki, you can impart energy to each one of these chakras and also correct any imbalances that may exist.

Here is a brief overview of these seven chakras:

THE FIRST CHAKRA – THE ROOT CHAKRA OR THE MULADHARA CHAKRA:

The first chakra is often referred to as your foundation chakra, earth chakra or the root chakra. It is located near the base of your spine, close to the pubic bone. It faces down towards your feet and connects you to the Earth. It is responsible for your basic urges such as hunger, thirst, sexual desires and the will to survive. It is also responsible for all fear and inhibitions. It holds together your talent and potential. By using Reiki power to energize this Chakra, you are also releasing your inner talent and potential. The physical organs associated with this Chakra are the rectum, the large intestine and the kidney.

THE SECOND CHAKRA – THE SACRAL CHAKRA OR THE 'HARA' CHAKRA:

The second chakra is also referred to as the Sacral chakra or the "Hara" chakra or, simply, the Abdomen chakra. In Sanskrit, it is called as the *Svadhisthana*. "Sva", in Sanskrit, means "of self" and "adhishthana" means "resting upon" or "abode". The word "adhastha" also means "inferior".

Therefore, this chakra is where your lower self generally rests. It can also be described as a worldly person's ego drive – it drives the immediate goals that will satisfy the ego. It is located at the very base of your spinal column and navel and serves as a focal point for your feelings, sexuality, creativity and movement.

Free flow of energy in this chakra will empower you to access your self-healing power along with your ability to have sensual pleasure. Any blockages in this chakra could lead to sexual guilt, unwanted addictions and obsessive behavior.

THE THIRD CHAKRA – THE SOLAR CHAKRA OR THE MANIPURA

The third chakra, also called the abundance chakra is regarded as your seat of power to achieve. It is the storehouse of energy and empowers you to achieve more. This chakra is located in your stomach just above the navel and is related to your power of digestion. The transformation of food to energy happens in this chakra. Blockages in this area could lead to issues with ego, power play or ambition.

THE FOURTH CHAKRA – THE HEART CHAKRA OR THE ANAHATA

The fourth Chakra is also called the Heart chakra. The Sanskrit name for this Chakra is *Anahata*. In Sanskrit, "*Anahata*" means "unhurt" or "unstruck".

At a tangible level, the name suggests that our heart should be made so strong that it remains unhurt or unscathed during all the trials and tribulations of life. This is the most powerful chakra and is considered to be the seat of the human soul. It is responsible for higher emotions such as love, compassion, spirituality, faith, etc.

This chakra is also the seat of your insecurity and fear such as despair, disappointment, loneliness, etc.

Imbalances in this chakra can manifest as insensitivity, lack of compassion and humanity. Reiki power enables free flow of energy in the chakra so that such feelings do not appear.

THE FIFTH CHAKRA – THE THROAT CHAKRA OR THE VISHUDDHA

In Sanskrit, this chakra is often referred to as Vishuddha. "Vishuddha" means "completely pure". This refers to the purity that emerges in your being after going through the grinding wheels of the experiences of the four chakras below the Throat chakra. After your lower chakras have been refined and after you have started experiencing unconditional Love, a new you starts to emerge. This new self of yours has an innate understanding of the law of karma and thus develops patience and equanimity under all circumstances. Your awareness at this chakra is the beginning of the deep dive that is about to happen in the infinite ocean of calmness, stillness and peace.

The throat chakra is the power of patience, understanding and self-expression. It also serves as the bridge between the feelings of the heart chakra and the rationality of the third eye. It is associated with your inborn capability to express, judge, communicate or create. The parts of body that are connected with the fifth Chakra are the parathyroid and the thyroid gland, arms, hands, neck and shoulders.

Blockages in this chakra are manifested as communication blocks or as blockages in creativity. Energizing this chakra through Reiki helps in enhancing communication skills as well as elevating the metabolic rate.

THE SIXTH CHAKRA – THE THIRD EYE CHAKRA OR THE AJNA

The sixth chakra is also called the Brow chakra or the Third Eye chakra. It is referred to as *Ajna* in Sanskrit. "*Ajna*" means command.

It signifies self-knowledge or spiritual genius. In a spiritually evolved person, the third eye chakra is the command center of the mind and the body. Opening of this chakra leads to spiritual genius as compared to the Solar chakra which turns you into a material genius.

This chakra is also called the center of your self-knowledge and intuition.

Sometimes, before something happens, you come to know about it. You can figure out what will happen even if you lack physical evidence to support your thoughts. Sometimes, your conscious mind is unable to detect certain things that exist as is. These can be detected by your power of intuition – or the sixth chakra.

At a physical level, this chakra is associated with the pituitary gland that is responsible for growth and development.

Reiki power can energize this Chakra to convert you into a spiritual genius.

THE SEVENTH CHAKRA – THE CROWN CHAKRA OR THE SAHASRARA

This Chakra is the seat of the formless consciousness - the supreme Almighty where all chakras become one - the multiple states of intelligences of different chakras merge into one integrated consciousness. Yoga thus happens.

In more definable terms, the *Sahasrara* is your seat of wisdom, enlightenment or pure consciousness. Your universal self is greater than you – it goes much beyond your physical self and is seated in the crown chakra.

A balanced and healthy seventh chakra implies a healthy spiritual life. The awareness that connects you with all things is a result of your balanced *Sahasrara*. You communicate with the Absolute though this chakra.

A closed seventh chakra indicates that you do not have interest in any kind of spiritual pursuit.

Reiki power prevents blockages in this chakra which may manifest as impulsiveness, rigidity in thoughts, depression, etc.

ENERGIZING CHAKRAS THROUGH REIKI

Reiki can be used to heal imbalances in any of the above seven chakras. By placing your hand over the seat of these seven chakras, you can channelize the flow of energy into that particular area and healing can take place. Sometimes, you may not be aware about the specific chakra that may need treatment. In this scenario, placing your hand over each one of these chakras will ensure that the imbalance gets rectified. Remember, Reiki energy is intelligent and flows to the areas where it is needed most.

MEDITATION AND REIKI

Meditation can be termed as the process of channelizing your thoughts or turning your attention to a specific part of body, mind or spirit inside or outside yourself. It plays an important role in self-healing and enables you to understand yourself and the Divine guidance. It is just a mechanism that allows you to build full concentration on a particular task and eliminate all distractions.

Once you are attuned to Reiki, you can begin practicing certain meditations that will ensure that your chakras are well balanced. These meditations also make your aware of the relationship that exists between your mind and body and therefore, helps in bringing them together. Meditation ensures that all blockages and imbalances are corrected via the flow of life force energy. It helps you experience ultimate peace and harmony – something like you have never experienced before!

Each chakra has a particular type of energy that is unique to that particular chakra. By performing meditation along with certain visualization and affirmation techniques, you can cleanse your chakras and open them up to receive life force energy.

In order to practice this chakra balancing meditation, you would need to find a quiet and secluded place. You must try and make enough time for meditation. The recommended time is half an hour a day. Put out the dog, switch off your phone and do everything else required to make sure that you do not get disturbed. Create your sacred space before you begin your meditation practice. Here is one of the simplest, yet impactful Reiki meditation techniques:

- Sit upright in a chair or in *Sukhasana* and close your eyes. Hold your hands in front of your chest in a 'Namaste' position and let the soles of your feel join together.

- Use the power of your intent to heal and unconditional love in order to connect to the Reiki energy within yourself.

- Visualize white light originating from your fingers.

- Now visualize your third eye chakra, experience unconditional love in the third eye chakra and meditate on it.

- Next, enable the unconditional love of Reiki move up as a bright light above your crown chakra. Bring your awareness back to the third eye chakra.

- Relax and release your thoughts on completing this meditation.

- Let warmth and peace move through your body. Experience the magical healing energy travel into ad through your body.

- After you have completed this meditation, imagine yourself being encircled by white light from head to toe. This white light acts as an energy shield that is going to protect you from any negative energy that may be trying to block the flow of energy through your body.

- Take a few deep breaths and move your toes, fingers, hands, legs and then slowly turn your attention towards your eyes. Open your eyes slowly and come out of the meditative state knowing that Reiki energy is flowing through all your chakras and will keep you healthy on all levels.

Let us look at some of the benefits that meditation has to offer:

INCREASED FOCUS: Irrespective of whether you are practicing a few minutes of meditation per day or indulging in a full day of meditative practice, your focus is bound to improve. This is primarily a result of regression of stress hormones in the body which when present force your brain to move in all possible directions. Meditation empowers you to understand when your mind is wandering and provide you the opportunity to correct it.

DECREASED ANXIETY: Well, meditation equals reduction in stress hormones and hence decreased anxiety. That's no rocket science!

Wait! There's more to it!

As you meditate, you loosen the connections of neural pathways that lead to your medial prefrontal cortex. The medial prefrontal cortex is the part of the brain that is responsible for processing information that impacts you directly such as an upsetting or a frightening moment.

Loosening this link via meditation enables you to look at the situation in a more rational manner.

ENHANCED CREATIVITY: Ample research has been conducted to prove that people who meditate are more creative and also open to new ideas.

ELEVATED MEMORY: When you meditate, you will be able to filter out all the distractions. This means you will be able to recall the stuff that you want to remember and filter out the stuff that does not need to be remembered.

INCREASED COMPASSION: People who practice meditation are more compassionate and empathetic towards others.

DECREASED STRESS: Studies suggest that mindfulness meditation leads to a substantial decrease in stress levels and as a result, lesser visits to the doctor.

CURE INSOMNIA TOO: That's correct! Meditation has the potential to cure chronic insomnia too. All you need is thirty minutes of dedicated practice each day.

MEDITATION CAN CHANGE YOUR BRAIN!Yes – meditation can change your brain and this is in fact, one of the greatest benefits of meditation. It decreases mind wandering, preserves an aging brain, elevates concentration levels and improves self-control.

SPECIFIC BENEFITS OF REIKI MEDITATION:

Here are some specific benefits of Reiki meditation:

- It brings about a deep sense of relaxation.

- It dissolves all energy blocks.

- It accelerates the natural healing process of wounds, etc.

- It changes negative training and behavior.

- It releases emotional wounds.

- It demolishes all disease.

HAND POSITIONS FOR HEALING

Reiki is all about transfer of energy from the master to the recipient through use of hands. It is therefore important to learn the various hand positions used to treat individuals using Reiki energy. The hand positions used in the West are slightly different from those used in traditional Reiki. The ones in the West have been introduced by Mrs. Takata.

You can treat all your seven chakras by placing your hands on the part of the body that is referred to as the seat of the chakra. Different hand positions are used to treat your own self and to treat others. The leg and feet positions were not a part of the traditional hand positions practiced in earlier days. They were introduced earlier in order to make the treatment more comprehensive. The feet are important organs responsible for holding the reflexes of your entire body.

HAND POSITIONS USED FOR SELF-TREATMENT

Head 1 position:

In Head 1 position, you are required to keep your right and left hands together in order to cover your eyes. This position is typically used to treat problems related to your third eye chakra. All problems related to ear, nose, throat, sinus, stress, hormonal imbalances, etc. are treated through use of this position.

Head 2 position:

In the Head 2 position, you are required to keep right and left wrists side by side and place the palms of each hands over the temples. This position is typically used to treat headaches, fatigue, immune deficiencies, problems related to pituitary gland, brain problems, problems related to nervous system, etc.

Head 3 position:

In the Head 3 position, the hands are placed on either side of the head as they lightly cup the ears. This position is extremely effective in treating any ear, nose, throat disorders or issues related to balance.

Head 4 position:

In the Head 4 position, the hands are placed behind the head in order to cover the back of the head. This position is used to treat tension, cold, problems related to the head and the neck, problems related to the spinal cord, etc.

Body 1 position:

To heal using this position, you should form a tent above your throat by holding your hands and fingers together. Your hands and fingers should not touch your throat. This problems heals problems related to worry, communication, the thymus gland, thyroid gland and the throat.

Body 2 position:

To heal using this position, you must hold your hands together and cover your collar bone as well as breast bone. This position will heal problems related to acceptance along with bronchitis, asthma, lungs, throat, etc.

Body 3 position:

To heal using this position, you must place your hands side by side over the upper part of your breasts. This position helps in treating problems related to the heart, thymus, lungs, emotional disturbances and circulation.

Body 4 position:

This position is used to specifically heal your Solar Plexus Chakra. To heal using this position, you must place your hands together under your breast, above the lower ribs. This position helps in treating your lungs, spleen, pancreas, liver, gall bladder and sternum. It is immensely helpful in treating digestive disorders.

Body 5 position:

To heal using this position, you must place both hands together over the stomach region, just above your navel. This position energizes the spleen, liver, kidneys, gall bladder, adrenal glands and digestive organs. It is considered to be an awesome therapy for people suffering from depression.

Body 6 position:

To experience healing using this position, you must place your hands over your pubic bone along your groin. This position is extremely helpful in treating reproductive organs, adrenal glands, testicles, ovaries, urinary bladder and kidneys. It helps in fighting fatigue and addresses weight loss issues too.

Back 3 position:

In order to heal yourself using this position, you must bring your hands together behind you and place it over the middle of your back, just above the kidneys. This position helps in treating relationship issues and also energizes the lungs, heart, adrenals and lymph nodes.

Back 4 position:

To experience healing using this position, you must bring your hand together behind you, and place them gently over your lower back, just over your waist. This position helps in treating mental problems and relationship issues. It also helps in revitalizing the digestive and reproductive organs.

Legs 1 position:

To heal using this position, place your hands on your knee cap – one hand over it and another just below it. This needs to be done separately for right and left knees. This position helps in removing energy blocks in the lower part of your body along with knee, neck and head injuries. It also makes you more flexible in your mind.

Leg 2 position:

To heal using this position, you must bring both your hands together over your ankle. This must first be done for right ankle and then for left ankle. This position is helpful in treating the throat, pelvis, thyroid, neck and lymph.

Leg 3 position:

This position has a calming impact and involves covering your foot with both your hands – using one hand above the foot and another to cover the sole of the foot. Repeat this for other foot too.

HAND POSITIONS TO TREAT OTHERS

If you intend to treat others, request them to be dressed in comfortable, loose clothing. Make them lie on a couch in a comfortable position and help them remove any metallic jewelry or belt that they are wearing. Remember, it is not important to place your hands over a client's body. You may simply hover your hands a few inches above their body and still get the same result.

Here are a few hand positions that you can try:

Head 1 position:

In order to heal others using this position, bring your hands together to cover the lowest part of your recipients face. Your thumbs should touch below the nose and you should not touch the eyes of the client – this can be extremely discomforting. This position is helpful in treating the third eye chakra along with lymphatic diseases, hormonal disorders and general ear, nose and throat problems.

Head 2 position:

To treat a client using this position, you must bring your hands together with wrists placed side by side. You must then place your hands over the client's temples. This position is extremely impactful in treating nervous problems, hormonal deficiencies, fatigue and tension related problems.

Head 3 position:

To heal using this position, place your hands at the sides of your clients head, lightly cupping their ears. This position is extremely effective in treating ear, nose and throat problems along with problems related to balance and orientation.

Head 4 position:

To heal using this position, slide your hands below the client's head and cup it with both hands. This position is helpful in treating anxiety, stress, neck, back and spinal problems.

Body 1 position:

In order to use this position, bring your hands and fingers together to form a tent above the throat of the client. Do not touch their throat though. This position will help in treating communication issues as well as issues of the thymus, thyroid and parathyroid.

Body 2 position:

To treat with this position, you must bring your hands together and place it over the collar bone or breast bone of your client. This position will treat lungs, bronchitis, and throat and thymus issues.

Body 3 position:

To heal a client using this position, it is advisable to bring your hands together and place them just above or below your recipient's breasts, without touching them. Problems related to immune as well as the circulatory system can be treated via this position.

Body 4 position:

To heal a client using this position, simply bring your hands together and place them under your clients breast, and above their lower ribs. This position helps in treating your lungs, spleen, pancreas, liver, gall bladder and sternum. It is immensely helpful in treating digestive disorders.

Body 5 position:

To heal using this position, you must place both hands together over your client's stomach region, just above your navel. This position energizes the spleen, liver, kidneys, gall bladder, adrenal glands and digestive organs. It is considered to be an awesome therapy for people suffering from depression.

Body 6 position:

To experience healing using this position, you must place your hands over your client's pubic bone along their groin region. This position is extremely helpful in treating reproductive organs, adrenal glands, testicles, ovaries, urinary bladder and kidneys. It helps in fighting fatigue and addresses weight loss issues too.

Back 1 position:

Get your client to sit comfortably on a chair and place your hands gently behind their neck. This position not only heals responsibility issues, but also treats headache, neck and shoulder problems.

Back 2 position:

To heal using this position, place your hands gently over your clients shoulder blades – on each sides. This can help in treating communication problems, depression and energize the lung and back region.

Back 3 position:

In order to heal a client using this position, you must get them to slightly lean forward. Then you must bring your hands together and place them over the middle of your client's back, just above their kidneys. This position helps in treating relationship issues and also energizes the lungs, heart, adrenals and lymph nodes.

Back 4 position:

To experience healing using this position, you must ask your client to lean forward and place your hand gently over their lower back, just over their waist. This position helps in treating mental problems and relationship issues. It also helps in revitalizing the digestive and reproductive organs.

Legs 1 position:

To heal using this position, ask your client to slowly raise their knee. Now place your hands on their knee cap – one hand over it and another just below it. This needs to be done separately for right and left knees. This position helps in removing energy blocks in the lower part of their body along with knee, neck and head injuries. It also makes them more flexible.

Leg 2 position:

To heal using this position, you must slide your hands under your client's ankle. Lay one hand above the ankle and the other below it. Do this separately for both ankles. This position is helpful in treating the throat, pelvis, thyroid, neck and lymph.

Leg 3 position:

This position has a calming impact and involves covering your client's foot with both your hands – using one hand above the foot and another to cover the sole of the foot. Repeat this for other foot too.

USING THE POWER OF REIKI TO ATTRACT ANYTHING THAT YOU WANT!

Well, experiencing abundance and prosperity is your birthright, isn't it?

And Reiki power can help you experience it to perfection.

Let us first take a minute to visualize what these two words mean to you.

Take two separate pieces of paper and write 'prosperity' on one piece and 'abundance' on another. Now, take a deep breath, relax, close your eyes and meditate upon one word at a time.

Prosperity – what do you visualize when you say this word…. when you feel this word….

Write down all that you can visualize.

Move to the next word – **Abundance!**

What do you visualize now?

Write down all that you can visualize – it could be money, power, fame, steady career, joyful marriage, amazing girlfriend, etc.

And now, let the Reiki energy flow through each of these words. Use this energy to tap into the unlimited supply of abundance and prosperity – use it to get anything that you want!

Develop your faith and belief in the Divine power – you are consciously being guided by a divine power that is much more wise, loving, intelligent and conscious. This Divine

Power is greater than anything else and guides and supports you – you may wish to call it God, Supreme, Absolute, Divine Light or anything that you choose to!

Integrating Reiki into your daily life can enable you to reach your true potential and experience greater progress. It can help you achieve anything that you want in life!

Try and bring this goodness to the world by passing it to as many people as you can. You are after all transforming the world – you are becoming the energy magnet who is now responsible for bringing prosperity and abundance in so many lives!

With Reiki, the possibilities are unlimited!

45695640R10035

Made in the USA
Middletown, DE
19 May 2019